# ROME

## COMPUTERIZED RECONSTRUCTION
## OF SITES AND MONUMENTS

# Electa

*Texts and photographs*
Luca Mozzati

*Editorial supervision*
Silvia Riboldi, Lucia Soncin

*Editing*
Annamaria Beltrami

*Drawings*
Alberto Ipsilanti, Silvana Ghioni

Translated from the Italian by Felicity Lutz and Susan Ann White for Scriptum, Rome

*Graphic and cartographic page layout*
Grafocart di Roberto Capra

*Photolithography*
Graphoset

*Organization and production*
Fabio Ratti Editoria S.r.l. - corso Monforte 16, Milano

www.electaweb.it

Reprint 2004
First Edition 2001

This volume was printed for Mondadori Electa S.p.A.
at Editoriale Lloyd s.r.l. Trieste, in the year 2004

# CONTENTS

# HISTORICAL EVENTS AND URBAN DEVELOPMENT
## 1. From the founding of the city to the birth of the Republic

"Throughout the world, wherever two important roads cross or a bridge exists, people stop. And a market springs up"; this is how the settlement that was to become Rome was born and developed. It could not have existed without the Tiber, which has been the pivotal element in city planning for thirty centuries. The existence of a ford in the vicinity of the Tiber Island made this the ideal meeting place for two major arteries: the salt road that led from the Tyrrhenian Sea to the Adriatic, and the road linking Etruria to Magna Graecia. The first settlements came into being at this ford in the Bronze Age (14th century BC), a few centuries earlier than the village of huts on the Palatine Hill dating from between the 9th and 8th century BC, which antedated the traditional date of the founding of the city, 21 April 753 BC. The importance of the ford, and the subsequent bridge, is underlined by the fact that it was considered sacred, which in the archaic period compensated for the lack of juridical norms. It is not a mere coincidence that the *pontifex*, the magistrate in charge of its protection, was to remain for centuries one of the most important figures in city life. At the end of the

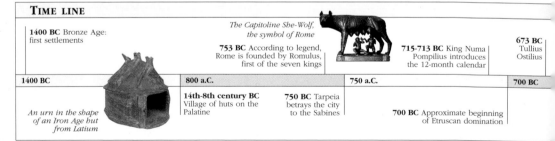

**TIME LINE**

| | | | |
|---|---|---|---|
| **1400 BC** Bronze Age: first settlements | *The Capitoline She-Wolf, the symbol of Rome* | **715-713 BC** King Numa Pompilius introduces the 12-month calendar | **673 BC** Tullius Ostilius |
| | **753 BC** According to legend, Rome is founded by Romulus, first of the seven kings | | |
| **1400 BC** | **800 a.C.** | **750 a.C.** | **700 BC** |
| *An urn in the shape of an Iron Age hut from Latium* | **14th-8th century BC** Village of huts on the Palatine  **750 BC** Tarpeia betrays the city to the Sabines | **700 BC** Approximate beginning of Etruscan domination | |

bridge, in the valley between the Capitol and the Palatine, the vegetable and cattle markets sprang up (later to become the *Forum Olitorium* and *Forum Boarium*). The need to control this crossroads became of vital importance to the Etruscan cities, whose products were sold in Magna Graecia and the Mediterranean area via the major trade centres in Campania.

During the early centuries Rome was governed by the legendary "Seven Kings", some of whom were definitely Etruscan, who foreshadowed a kind of monarchy controlled more or less directly by northern neighbours. In the 6th century, at the time of the Tarquins, the city became a unified religious and political organism, defined by a sacred boundary, the *pomerium*, and subdivided into four sectors, alongside which were located some "service" areas, excluded from the administrative divisions, such as the acropolis on the Capitol that had a sacred function, the *Forum Boarium* and *Forum Olitorium* used for trading, and the Aventine Hill where the "foreign" comunities resided. During the 6th century BC the first walls – of which a few vestiges remain – were erected and the city boasted a large public area used for trading, the Forum, where the land between the inhabited hills, which had previously been marshy and used as a cemetery, had been reclaimed by digging a drainage canal known as the *Cloaca Maxima*. This was also the site of the political centre (*comitium*), the king's residence (*regia*) and the major sanctuaries.

| | | | 507 BC War against the Etruscans. Horatius Cocles defends the bridge over the Tiber | |
|---|---|---|---|---|
| **640 BC** Ancus Martius | **600 BC** Likely date of the construction of the *Cloaca Maxima* | **565 BC** Likely date of the construction of the Servian Walls around the seven hills of Rome | **534 BC** Servius Tullius is killed    **510 BC** Consecration of the Temple of Jupiter on the Capitol | |
| **650 BC** | | **600 BC** | **550 BC** | **500 BC** |
| **659 BC** Rome destroys its rival city Alba Longa | **616 BC** Tarquinius Priscus, first Etruscan king. Construction of the Forum and the Circus Maximus | **578 BC** Servius Tullius, Etruscan king | **510 BC** L. J. Brutus expels the Etruscans from Rome and establishes the Republic    **506 BC** The Sabines defeat the Etruscan King Porsenna and gain hegemony in Latium | |

*Lucius Junius Brutus*

## 2. The centuries of the Republic

In 509 BC Tarquin the Proud, last of the Etruscan kings, was expelled from the city and a Republican government was established. According to tradition, this coincided with the gradual decline of Etruscan power, which had been gravely weakened by defeats suffered at the hands of the Greeks, Carthaginians and Cumaeans. During that same period Rome began to establish itself in the Mediterranean area and built the most important archaic temple, the Capitoline Temple of Jupiter; both these facts evince its political independence and autonomous development. In the first half of the 5th century BC intense construction work was carried out on the monumental edifices in the Forum, where the *Regia* was converted into a cult building for the religious rites performed by the *rex sacrificulus*, an indication of the continuity of the king's sacred office. In 456 BC a law assigned the Aventine to plebeian families, thus promoting the hill's development.

Internal unrest and the virtually constant wars against neighbouring populations brought urban development to a halt and it was only after the Gauls set fire to the city in 390 BC – the famous episode of the Capitoline geese giving the alarm became legendary – that reconstruction work started. A new and more imposing city wall (inappropriately known today as the Servian Wall) began to be built in 378 BC, and its 11-kilometre length surrounded the whole city except the Capitol, which

## TIME LINE

**499 BC** Battle against the Latins; the Temple of Castor and Pollux is built to commemorate the victory

**445 BC** *Lex Canuleia:* the ban on marriage between patricians and plebeians is abolished

**390 a.C.** Rome is invaded by the Gauls: the geese on the Capitol raise the alarm before the attack

**365 BC** Construction of the Via Nomentana, from Rome to Mentana, the Tiburtina, from Rome to Tivoli, the Salaria from Rome to Porto Ascoli

**330 BC** Arch of Janus

**500 BC**       **450 BC**       **400 BC**       **350 BC**

*The three columns of the Temple of Castor and Pollux in the Roman Forum*

**456 BC** The Aventine is made by law a residential area for plebeian families

**396 BC** Definitive victory over Veii, Rome's Etruscan rival

**378 BC** The Servian Wall is built

**498 BC** Temple of Saturn

was independently fortified.

During subsequent years nearly all the buildings in the Forum were renovated or newly constructed. Towards the end of the 4th century BC the censor Appius Claudius Ciecus built the first aqueduct, which was 16 kilometres long, could supply the city with 73,000 cubic metres of water every day and was situated at the beginning of the famous Via Appia, the *regina viarum* (queen of roads), leading to Campania where Roman expansion was concentrated. As the territory controlled by Rome gradually extended, the city acquired the features of a centre of power, which were to remain its hallmark. The victory over Carthage in 202 BC and the control of the Mediterranean suddenly raised Rome to the status of a major metropolis, and set it within a context deeply permeated by eastern and Hellenistic culture. There followed a period of great urban renewal on a grandiose scale never seen before, both in practical and prestigious works. Huge warehouses and port facilities were constructed on the Tiber; imposing markets, long rows of porticoes and magnificent basilicas were built. Soon after the cultural transformation resulting from contact with Hellenistic culture, the taboo that prohibited the building of permanent places for entertainment was broken. The most prominent personages vied with each other to offer the city magnificent brick edifices to replace the earlier wooden structures, using the immense wealth accumulated in military campaigns and in their public capacities, from the concentration of land ownership

**298-290 BC**
Third Samnite War

**264-241 BC** First Punic War against Carthage

**220 BC** Construction of the Via Flaminia linking Rome to the Adriatic

**187 BC** The Via Emilia from Rimini to Piacenza

**171-168 BC** Third Macedonian War. The victory over the Macedonians completes the Roman conquest of Greece

**154 BC** The Via Cassia from Rome to Arezzo

| 300 BC | 250 BC | 200 BC | 150 BC |

**312 BC** The Via Appia and the first Roman aqueduct the *Aqua Appia*

**241 BC** Construction of the Via Aurelia linking Rome to Liguria

**218-201 BC** Second Punic War. Scipio Africanus defeats the Carthaginians

**149-146 BC** Third Punic War: destruction of Carthage

*The Via Appia Antica*

*The Roman Forum*

and the expansion of commercial enterprise.

The drainage system, road and water supply networks were improved by such major constructions as the *Pons Aemilius*, the first stone bridge to be built. Costly and highly prized imported marble was used in the place of local travertine or brickwork in the temples; there was an increase in the number of luxury residences with courtyards and very elegant suburban villas, preferably decorated with Greek works of art, procured by any means and at any price; while the housing requirements of a rapidly growing population were met by creating *insulae*, buildings similar to modern low-cost apartment blocks with stores or workshops on the ground floor and residential apartments on the upper floors, which were often built with shoddy materials, were unhealthy, and rented to the plebs.

The celebration of a power, which ambition and circumstances rendered personal rather than of service to the public, led to the invention of the triumphal arch and the kind of individual portraiture which was Hellenistic in origin, but reached its height of realistic expression among the Romans in the depiction of true likenesses. It portrayed the face of a political class that strictly adhered to its own ethical

*The Temple of Fortuna Virilis*

## TIME LINE

**142 BC** First brick bridge over the Tiber the *Pons Aemilius*

**133-120 BC** The Gracchi are killed because of agrarian reforms

**111-105 BC** War against Jugurtha. Victory of the consul Caius Marius

**100 BC** Caius Marius defeats the Cimbri at the battle of the Campi Raudii

**101 BC** Temple of Fortuna Virilis in the Forum Boarium

**150 BC**

**100 BC**

**144 BC** The aqueduct of *Aqua Marcia* 92 km long

**109 BC** Ponte Milvio over the Tiber

**135-132 BC** First Slave War

**103-100 BC** Second Slave War

**91-88 BC** Social War. The Italic allies (*socii*) demand equal rights. Finally Rome grants them Roman citizenship

*A section of Roman aqueduct*

codes, which were displayed with an almost fierce pride. During this period the power of the Senate was gradually undermined by great, ambitious, unscrupulous generals who prepared the transition from the Republican government to the Principate. These included Marius, Silla, Caesar, Crassus and Pompey, who were all linked to the army by a system of self-interest and favoritism.

After the bloodbath of the Social War (91-88 BC), in which the Italics fought the Romans to obtain equal rights, under Silla's dictatorship (82-80 BC) urban development became a state affair and monumental building definitively acquired the ritual aspect that transformed temples, squares and colonnades into a dazzling backdrop for displays of power.

*The Forum of Caesar*

| | | | | |
|---|---|---|---|---|
| **88-85 BC** First Mithridatic War | **70 BC** Publius Virgilius Marone is born | **60 BC** Rome is governed by Pompey, Crassus and Caesar (first triumvirate) | **46 BC** Caesar constructs the Forum that bears his name | |
| **76-63 BC** Second Mithridatic War | | **58-50 BC** Caesar's expedition to Gaul | | |
| | | | **50 BC** | |
| **82-80 BC** Silla's dictatorship | **63 BC** Catiline conspiracy | **55 BC** First permanent theatre in Rome | **49 BC** Caesar crosses the Rubicon and enters Rome. The civil war between Caesar and Pompey begins | |
| **71 BC** Third Slave War. The slave revolt led by Spartacus is quashed by Crassus and Pompey | **65 BC** Horace is born | **51 BC** Caesar conquers Gaul | | |

## 3. The Rome of Augustus

Caesar's ambitious project, which included the urbanization of Campus Martius, the deviation of the course of the Tiber, and other interventions that were to have a profound influence on the future development of the city, was temporarily brought to a halt by his assassination in 44 BC. Nonetheless, the process that was to transform the ancient city of the Roman aristocracy into an immense, modern metropolis in the Hellenistic mould and capable of playing its role as *caput mundi* was by now unstoppable. The "moderate" reform promoted with subtle, political acumen by Octavian Augustus, proclaimed *primus inter pares* (first among equals) after the grim struggle against Caesar's assassins and then against Mark Antony that came to an end in 31 BC, reached even further. Administrative and urban organization was changed by dividing the city into fourteen sectors. The Campus Martius was subjected to the most extensive "official" interventions carried out by Augustus and Agrippa, his righthand man, with the aim of winning over the emerging classes. Some of the major Roman monuments were built at this time and these included the Pantheon and the emperor's huge mausoleum that still survive today and made the area the site of the celebration of the new image of power, of the figure of the *princeps* (leader) and his dynasty.

The old Forum was also greatly transformed by the construction of the temple dedicated to the *Deus Julius*

---

**TIME LINE**

*A detail of the frieze on the Ara Pacis with figures in procession*

**31 BC** Battle of Actium. Octavian defeats Antony and Cleopatra

**27 BC** Octavian receives the title of Augustus and re-establishes the Republic; he constructs his Mausoleum and the Imperial Forum

**13 BC** The Ara Pacis is erected to celebrate the peace that Augustus has brought to the Empire

**27 BC** Marcus Agrippa constructs the Pantheon

50 a.C. | 0

**44 BC** Caesar becomes dictator for life, but is assassinated by Brutus and Cassius

*The Mausoleum of Augustus*

**11 BC** Theatre of Marcellus

**19 BC** Marcus Agrippa constructs the aqueduct of the Acqua Vergine, the last basin of which was used to create the Trevi Fountain in the 18th century

**4 BC** Jesus Christ is born, 4 years before the date calculated by the monk Dionysius Exiguus

while the Forum built by Caesar and dominated by the *Temple of Venus Genitrix*, obviously of the *Gens Julia* and hence of the dictator himself, whose potential deification in life and establishment of monarchic power it stressed, was flanked by an even more imposing forum, with the magnificent *Temple of Mars Ultor*. The iconographic scheme of the whole complex was typically Augustan, since the whole history of the Republic was expressed through images of its mythical and real protagonists, finishing by identifying it with the history of the *Gens Julia*, from Aeneas to Romulus, with their divine parents Venus and Mars, thus justifying the existing empire as being the inevitable conclusion of the history of the Republic. In the centre of the Forum stood the statue of Augustus in his triumphal chariot, the man of providence, worthy of receiving his glorious inheritance and of guiding the now "eternal" city towards new goals. Extremely concerned with the symbolic significance of his actions, Augustus chose to live on the Palatine in a relatively unpretentious house that was however located in an area dominated by the Temple of Apollo and by the Sanctuary of the *Magna Mater*, Cybele, and according to tradition, near the site of Romulus's residence. This was the last piece in the mythical backdrop of the new state.

*St. Peter*

| 4 AD Augustus adopts his stepson Tiberius to ensure succession | 14 AD Augustus dies, Tiberius succeeds him | 19 AD Germanicus, Tiberius' likely successor, dies mysteriously | 41 AD Reign of Claudius, brother of Germanicus | 42 AD The apostle Paul arrives in Rome |
|---|---|---|---|---|

**50 AD**

| 12 AD Map of the Roman Empire based on the indications of M. Vipsanius Agrippa | 37 AD Caligula has the obelisk now in Piazza San Pietro transported from Heliopolis | 50 AD Work begins on the construction of the port of Ostia at the mouth of the Tiber |
|---|---|---|

*Christ blessing (Stefaneschi Polyptych, Giotto)*

## 4. The city in the Imperial Era

The adoption of the eastern imperial cult, finally offered the West and its elites a perfect framework in which to stage and consolidate its prestige. Set within the established ritual system, the new cult gave both the individual and the community the possibility of contributing actively and systematically to the welfare of the state. The fire in 64 AD, during Nero's reign, which destroyed most of the city, provided the occasion for inevitable renewal, but financial resources were almost completely exhausted by the incredible undertaking of the construction of the *Domus Aurea* (Golden House), based on the model of the residences of Hellenistic and oriental sovereigns. It was the

Flavians who put into practice a policy of "public restitution" or returning land to the people and erected exceptional public buildings on the remains of the *Domus Aurea*, including the Colosseum. A few years later, Diocletian built the palace on the Palatine that established the definitive model for the imperial residence. Under Trajan (98-117 AD) the Empire reached its maximum expansion and Rome became the largest and most densely populated city in the ancient world (it is estimated to have had a population of between 6/700,000 and 1,000,000). Trajan was responsible for the last and most imposing of the Imperial Forums and the adjacent market, designed by the brilliant architect Apollodorus from Damascus. During the whole of the 2nd century AD until the beginning of the 3rd century

---

**TIME LINE**

*The Porta di San Sebastiano in the Aurelian Walls*

**64 AD** Under Nero a fire destroys the city

**After 81 AD** Arch of Titus

**113 AD** Apollodorus of Damascus creates Trajan's Forum

**118-125 AD** Hadrian reconstructs the Pantheon

**164-180 AD** The plague rages throughout the Roman Empire

**203 AD** Arch of Septimius Severus

**271-275 AD** Aurelian Walls

| 50 AD | 100 AD | 150 AD | 200 AD | 250 AD |
|---|---|---|---|---|

*The Colosseum*

**72 AD** Work begins on the Colosseum

**110 AD** Trajan extends the Circus Maximus

**117 AD** Hadrian becomes emperor. He builds his Tomb (Castel Sant'Angelo) and Hadrian's Villa at Tivoli

**193 AD** Aurelian Column

**212 AD** Roman citizenship is granted to all inhabitants of the Empire

**217 AD** The Baths of Caracalla are completed

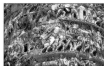
*A detail of the frieze decorating the Aurelian Column*

AD the city was extended and embellished with splendid monuments, including the Pantheon, Hadrian's huge mausoleum, and the Aurelian Column, which can all still be seen today. Between 212 and 216 AD Caracalla constructed the spectacular baths, alongside the complexes created by Agrippa, Nero, Titus and Trajan, followed by those by Diocletian and Constantine. In the mid-3rd century AD the situation rapidly deteriorated, when the crisis that had been latent for some time involved the Empire in a dramatic series of power struggles which were aggravated by the chronic economic recession and increasing pressure from the barbarian populations. The hasty construction of the Aurelian Walls (271-275 AD) both symbolically and concretely marked the end of Rome's period of expansion. Despite great building development under Diocletian (284-313 AD) and the ambitious projects begun by Maxentius (306-312 AD) and completed by Constantine (306-337 AD), the fortunes of ancient Rome were now waning. The founding of Constantinople, the new capital, confirmed this: now the centre of power was in the east. Thus the sack by the Goths of Alaric (410 AD) and later attacks by the Vandals in 455 AD and 472 AD anticipated an end that the removal of the last emperor Romulus Augustulus confirmed (476 AD).

*The Arch of Constantine*

| | | | | | | | |
|---|---|---|---|---|---|---|---|
| **298 AD** Work begins on the construction of the Baths of Diocletian | **315 AD** Dedication of the Arch of Constantine | | | | | | **476 AD** The West Roman Empire falls; Byzantium becomes the centre of the Empire |
| | | **330 AD** Constantinople made the new capital of the Empire | | **395 AD** Division of the Empire between Ravenna and Constantinople | | | |

| 300 AD | 350 AD | 400 AD | 450 AD | 500 AD |
|---|---|---|---|---|

| | | | | |
|---|---|---|---|---|
| **293 AD** Division of the Empire | | | **410 AD** Rome is sacked by the Goths led by Alaric | **455 AD** Rome is again sacked by the Vandals |
| **306-312 AD** Basilica of Maxentius | **313 AD** Edict of Milan. Freedom of worship for Christians | **380 AD** The Emperor Theodosius makes Christianity the official religion of the Roman Empire | | |

# KINGS, CONSULS AND EMPERORS

Rome had over 250 rulers in the 1,200 years between its foundation by Romulus and AD 476, when the last emperor was deposed by the German warrior, Odoacer. Romulus was the first of seven kings, overthrown in 509 BC when Rome became a Republic. Authority was held by two annually elected consuls, but provision was made for the appointment of a dictator in times of crisis. In 494 BC, the office of Tribune was set up to protect the plebeians from patrician injustice. Roman democracy, however, was always cosmetic. It was discarded completely in 27 BC, when absolute power was placed in the hands of Octavian.

*Lucius Junius Brutus*

*The Capitoline She-Wolf that evokes the legend of Romulus and Remus is a bronze statue dating from the 5th century BC in the Museo dei Conservatori*

**c. 715-673 BC** Numa Pompilius

**616-579 BC** Tarquinius Priscus

**c. 509 BC** Lucius Junius Brutus and Horatius Pulvillus

| 800 BC | 700 BC | 600 BC | 500 BC |
|---|---|---|---|
| **THE SEVEN KINGS** | | | **REPUBLIC** |
| 800 BC | 700 BC | 600 BC | 500 BC |

**c. 673-641 BC** Tullus Ostilius

**c. 579-534 BC** Servius Tullius

**c. 753-715 BC** Romulus

**c. 641-616 BC** Ancus Martius

**534-509 BC** Tarquin the Proud

**456 BC** Lucius Quintus Cincinnatus

**205 a.C.** Scipio Africanus

*Scipio Africanus*

**45-44 BC** Julius Caesar dictator for life

*Julius Caesar*

**43-32 BC** Second Triumvirate of Mark Antony, Octavian and Lepidus

*Octavianus Augustus*

*Vespasian*

*Marcus Aurelius*

**63 BC** Cicero

**107-87 BC** Seven-Year Consulship of Marius

**122-121 BC** Caius Graccus

**218 BC** Quintus Fabius Maximus

**37-41 AD** Caligula

**14-37 AD** Tiberius

**27 BC -14 AD** Augustus

**69-79 AD** Vespasian

**79-81 AD** Titus

**81-96 AD** Domitian

**96-98 AD** Nerva

**161-180 AD** Marcus Aurelius

**180-192 AD** Commodus

**211-217 AD** Caracalla

**218-222 AD** Heliogabalus

**270-275 AD** Aurelian

**306-337 AD** Constantine (joint emperor with Maxentius **307-312 AD**)

**337-340 AD** Constantine II (joint emperor with Constantius II **337-361 AD**)

**361-363 AD** Julian the Apostate

| 400 BC | 300 BC | 200 BC | 100 BC | 0 | 100 AD | 200 AD | 300 AD | 400 AD |
|---|---|---|---|---|---|---|---|---|

**EMPIRE**

| 400 BC | 300 BC | 200 BC | 100 BC | 0 | 100 AD | 200 AD | 300 AD | 400 AD |
|---|---|---|---|---|---|---|---|---|

**133 BC** Tiberius Graccus

**81-80 BC** Silla

**70-63 BC** Pompey

**60-53 BC** Triumvirate of Julius Caesar, Pompey and Crassus

**396 BC** Marcus Furius Camillus

**41-54 AD** Claudius

**54-68 AD** Nero

**98-117 AD** Trajan

**117-138 AD** Hadrian

**138-161 AD** Antoninus Pius

**193-211 AD** Septimius Severus

**222-235 AD** Alexander Severus

**284-305 AD** Diocletian

**379-395 AD** Theodosius

**475-476 AD** Romulus Augustulus

*Trajan*

*Septimius Severus*

# CITY GUIDE

## The expansion of Rome from its founding to the fall of the Empire

The map shows the extension of the city of Rome from its origins to the fall of the West Roman Empire in 476 AD. According to legend Rome was founded by Romulus, one of the twins suckled by the she-wolf, in 753 BC. However, excavations near the Tiber Island, where a ford made it possible to cross the river, have brought to light the remains of settlements dating back to the Bronze Age (14th century BC). The city developed from this site, extending first towards the Palatine Hill where huts from the 9th-8th century BC have been discovered, then to the valley between the Capitol and the Palatine, where markets were situated; the foreign community resided on the Aventine Hill. In the 6th century BC the city was divided into four districts and surrounded by walls; the Forum was a meeting and trading place. In the 4th century BC, the Servian Wall was built; the Capitol had a separate defensive system. Under Augustus (1st century AD), the city was divided into fourteen districts and extended towards the Campus Martius, where major urban development took place. During Trajan's reign, from 98-117 AD, Rome became the largest and most densely populated urban centre (perhaps with a million inhabitants) in the ancient world. The Aurelian Walls, built between 271 and 275 AD, mark the boundary of the ancient city, which from that moment onwards entered a decline provoked by the crisis within the Empire and the transfer of the capital to Constantinople.

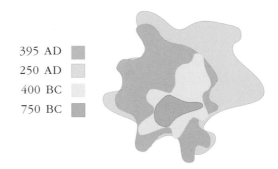

395 AD

250 AD

400 BC

750 BC

*Hadrian's Tomb (see pp. 82-83)*

*Ara Pacis (see pp. 92-93)*

*Pantheon (see pp. 80-81)*

VATICAN

CAMPO MARZIO

CASTRO PRETORIO

QUIRINAL

JANICULUM

CAPITOL

ESQUILINE

ROMAN FORUM

PALATINE

TRASTEVERE

FORUM BOARIUM

LATERAN

COELIAN

*Roman Forum (see pp. 22-37)*

AVENTINE

*Temple of Hercules Victor, Forum Boarium (see pp. 68-69)*

*Palatine and Colosseum (see pp. 38-55)*

# THE SACRED AREA OF SANT'OMOBONO

The original access to the Capitol was along a very evocative route steeped in history. At the crossroads between Via del Teatro Marcello and the ancient *Vicus Jugarius* the ruins of a small travertine portico can still be seen. This was perhaps the *Porticus Triumphalis*, through which triumphal processions passed on their way to the Capitol. Opposite lies the Sacred Area of Sant'Omobono. The excavations of 1937 brought to light finds of enormous importance as regards the history of the origins of Rome and the Republican Era. Beneath what is visible at ground level dating from the Imperial Era, six meters below the surface, pottery from the 14th century BC was found in a village that was probably the nucleus of Rome. The other strata contained finds from Ischia and Greece, dating from the Iron Age and the 8th century BC, which are evidence of relations existing at the time when the city was founded. The most significant monuments are the remains of the sanctuaries of *Fortuna* and *Mater Matuta*, built by Servius Tullius in the 6th century BC and destroyed at the end of that century at the same time as the traditional founding of the Republic, since they were the dynastic temples of the Etruscan kings. The reconstruction of the temples was undertaken by Camillus, after the capture of Veii (396 BC) that marked the definitive defeat of the Etruscans. After the fire of 213 BC the identical temples were once again completely reconstructed side by side, which is evidence of their enormous importance, as is proved by the rebuilding of the *Porticus Triumphalis* in the Imperial Era.

*The Church of Sant'Omobono with ruins from the Imperial Era*

*A vertical section of the sacred area of Sant'Omobono showing the strata of the excavations*

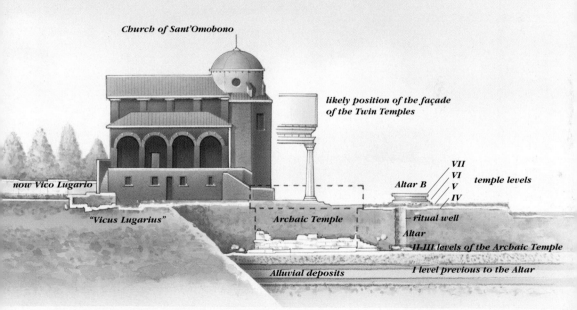

Church of Sant'Omobono

likely position of the façade
of the Twin Temples

now Vico Lugario

"Vicus Lugarius"

Archaic Temple

Altar B

VII
VI
V
IV

temple levels

ritual well

Altar

II-III levels of the Archaic Temple

Alluvial deposits

I level previous to the Altar

# THE CAPITOL

The hill does not have impressive vestiges of ancient Rome, when it played the role of the *Arx* (fortress) par excellence of the city. The most ancient settlements date from the Bronze Age (14th century BC) and bear out the tradition according to which the nucleus of Rome was founded by Saturn on the Capitoline Hill. In founding the city Romulus created a "bonded area" for refugees in the depression between the two hills, *Capitolium* and *Arx*, and called Asylum, where the piazza stands today. When the hill became an acropolis, the most venerated sanctuaries, the seat of government, the civic institutions and the archive were located there. On the site of the Church of S. Maria in Aracoeli rose the *Temple of Juno Moneta* or Juno the Admonisher, beside it stood the mint, and from it our word "money" originated. The most important building, however, was

*Santa Maria in Aracoeli*

the vast Capitoline Temple of Jupiter, the major centre of the state cult, dedicated to Jupiter the Best and Greatest, Juno and Minerva. This edifice, the highest achievement of archaic Rome, was begun by the Tarquins, but inaugurated in 509 BC. It was built on a north-south axis, measured 53 x 63 m and probably had three orders of six columns along the front to support the deep pronaos. The *cella* divided into three sections housed the three images of the gods. The ornate pediment was decorated with an impressive terracotta quadriga, the work of Vulca of Veii; the imposing remains are in the Museo dei Conservatori. After being destroyed by fire in 83 BC, it was partially rebuilt in marble, with the huge columns Silla ordered to be brought from the Temple of Olympic Zeus at Athens. It was reconstructed for the last time in Domitian's reign.

# THE ROMAN FORUM

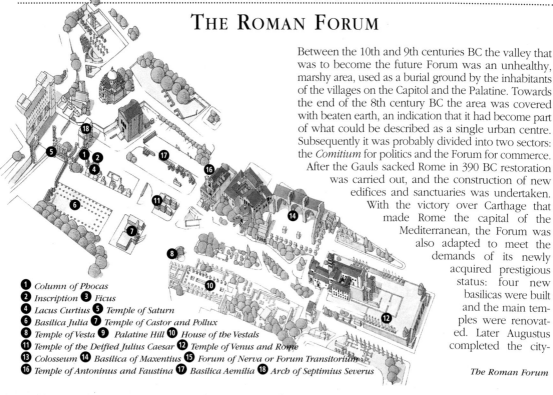

Between the 10th and 9th centuries BC the valley that was to become the future Forum was an unhealthy, marshy area, used as a burial ground by the inhabitants of the villages on the Capitol and the Palatine. Towards the end of the 8th century BC the area was covered with beaten earth, an indication that it had become part of what could be described as a single urban centre. Subsequently it was probably divided into two sectors: the *Comitium* for politics and the Forum for commerce. After the Gauls sacked Rome in 390 BC restoration was carried out, and the construction of new edifices and sanctuaries was undertaken. With the victory over Carthage that made Rome the capital of the Mediterranean, the Forum was also adapted to meet the demands of its newly acquired prestigious status: four new basilicas were built and the main temples were renovated. Later Augustus completed the city-

1 Column of Phocas
2 Inscription 3 Ficus
4 Lacus Curtius 5 Temple of Saturn
6 Basilica Julia 7 Temple of Castor and Pollux
8 Temple of Vesta 9 Palatine Hill 10 House of the Vestals
11 Temple of the Deified Julius Caesar 12 Temple of Venus and Rome
13 Colosseum 14 Basilica of Maxentius 15 Forum of Nerva or Forum Transitorium
16 Temple of Antoninus and Faustina 17 Basilica Aemilia 18 Arch of Septimius Severus

*The Roman Forum*

planning work begun by Silla and continued by Caesar. The construction of the Imperial Forums relegated the Republican Forum to the role of official, monumental backdrop destined to enhance the magnificence and prestige of the dynasty. The Forum served this purpose, though some alterations were made, throughout the Imperial Era, until 608 AD, when the column in honour of the Emperor Phocas, the last Roman monument, was erected. From then on, the area gradually became covered with earth and the monuments, with the exception of those that were Christianized, disappeared. By the Middle Ages the Forum had become the Campo Vaccino (cow field) and until the end of the 18th century the principal monuments were exploited as fortresses, quarries and sources of lime.

## The Basilica Aemilia

On the right of the *Via Sacra* (Sacred Way), facing the Capitol, are the ruins of the vast *Basilica Aemilia*, the only one of the four Republican basilicas to have survived. Built in 179 BC, it was restored several times and finally reconstructed by Augustus. The basilica, probably originating in the Hellenistic eastern Mediterranean

(*stoà basileios* = royal portico), was where the legal, commercial and political activities of the Forum were carried out under cover in bad weather. The floor plan of the large Republican basilica can be seen in an excavated section on the west side. The side facing the Forum, around 100 metres long, had two orders of 16 arches along the front and 16 shops on the ground floor. The inner hall (90 x 29 metres) could be accessed through three entrances. The remains of the coins that melted during the fire started by Alaric in 410 AD can be seen in the pavement. Beside the entrance steps stands a marble podium from the *Shrine of Venus Cloacina*, a sanctuary linked to the *Cloaca Maxima* that entered the Forum at this point. In front of the Curia is the site of the *Comitium*, the ancient political centre of the city. Still visible opposite the Curia is the small, square area known as the *Lapis Niger*, paved in black marble to indicate its funerary nature, and separated from the rest of the area by a white marble wall. According to tradition this is the site of Romulus's tomb. Dating from the reign of Silla, this pavement covers extremely ancient constructions that include the famous stone with the following Latin inscription dating from the 6th century BC: "He who violates this place will be delivered to the infernal gods".

*The Basilica Aemilia with the Curia, the Arch of Septimius Severus, the columns of the Temple of Saturn and the Tabularium in the background*

# The Curia

The large brick edifice is the Curia Julia, seat of the Senate, begun by Caesar, completed by Augustus, rebuilt by Diocletian, converted into a church in the 7th century AD, and restored in 1930-36. The imposing interior with its wooden ceiling is 21 m high, 18 m wide and 27 m long. The marble pavement is in part original. The seats of around 300 senators were located on the tiers. The central niche contained a statue of Victory. The building houses the so-called *plutei* of Trajan, which were perhaps part of a wall of the Forum, and whose fine reliefs represent a vivid picture of life in their depiction of the remission of citizens' tax debts by burning the registers and the introduction of *Alimenta*, which were low-interest agricultural loans.

*A detail of the decoration on the Arch of Septimius Severus*

# The Arch of Septimius Severus

This triumphal arch with three supporting arches originally surmounted by a bronze quadriga was erected in 203 AD. It is 21 m high, 23 m wide, and 11 m deep. The exterior with its strong chiaroscuro effect created by the columns in full relief is faced in marble. An inscription running round both sides of the attic dedicated to Septimius Severus and his sons Caracalla and Geta celebrates the victories over the Parthians. The reliefs include victories, various deities, a small frieze of the emperor's triumph, Roman soldiers with prisoners and four large panels depicting the campaigns against the Parthians. These deteriorated reliefs are in a narrative style that is very effective. Their arrangement in orders one above the other derives from the paintings executed to illustrate military campaigns that were borne during the triumphal processions of victorious generals.

*The Roman Forum with the few vestiges of the Temple of the Deified Julius Caesar (the podium) in the foreground*

# The Tabularium

The following buildings are situated on the slopes of the Capitoline Hill: the *Tabularium*, built by Silla in 78 BC as the state archive, whose imposing colonnaded structure was to influence all subsequent architecture; the *Temple of Concord* erected in 376 BC, of which only the brickwork podium remains; on its left the three beautiful remaining columns of the *Temple of Vespasian* on the corner of the hexastyle pronaos, constructed by Domitian in 81 AD; to the left of this, the *Porticus Deorum Consentium*, dating from the reign of Flavius but reconstructed in 367 AD, consists of eight adjoining rooms with twelve fluted cipollin columns along the front. Lower down stand the eight majestic granite columns with smooth shafts and Ionic capitals supporting the architrave of the hexastyle façade of the *Temple of Saturn*. It was built during the rule of the kings, and was reconstructed several times, the last being after the fire of 283 AD. A building in front of the temple housed the state treasury. On the left of the Arch of Septimius Severus is the semicircular tribune of the *Rostra*, from which the orators made their speeches, decorated with the beaks of ships captured from the Volsci at Anzio in 338 BC. On the left, the *Miliarium Aureum*, erected by Augustus, symbolically marked the spot where all the consular roads began. Opposite, on a high podium, stands the *Column of Phocas*, dedicated by the Senate in 608 AD to the emperor who had made a gift of the Pantheon to Pope Boniface IV. This column, dating from the 2nd-3rd century AD, was the last monument to be built in the Forum. The nearby trapezium-shaped area was probably the site of the *Lacus Curtius*, the last remaining vestige of marshland, that is linked to many legends, one of which recounts how, in obedience to an oracle, Marcus Curtius jumped into this lake on his horse.

*The imposing edifice of the Tabularium that housed the state archive with the columns of the Temples of Vespasian and Saturn, and, on the right, the Arch of Septimius Severus and the Column of Phocas*

# The Basilica Julia

On the other side of the Via Sacra stands the *Basilica Julia*, the largest and most magnificent edifice in the Forum (101 x 49 metres), erected by Caesar, reconstructed by Augustus and restored by Domitian after the fire of 283 AD. The great central hall (82 x 18 metres) was surrounded on all sides by a double row of brick and travertine pillars (partially reconstructed) that divided the area into five aisles. The steps and pavement still bear traces of games and drawings of statues carved into the stone by idlers of the time. On the other side of the *Vicus Tuscus* that indicates the presence of an Etruscan quarter, rises the huge podium of the *Temple of Castor and Pollux* with its three superb, surviving columns. Inaugurated in 484 BC, it was restored in 117 BC (the date of the podium), and finally by Tiberius in 6 AD (the date of the columns). This is a peripteral temple with eight columns along the front and eleven along the sides; it was used for Senate meetings and housed the office for controlling weights and measures. The enormous edifice on the right, known as the *Temple of Augustus*, dates from the Imperial Era. Nearby stands the *Fountain of Juturna* where Castor and Pollux are said to have watered their horses after the battle of Lake Regillus. The fine basin faced in marble dates from the 2nd century BC. Returning towards the Forum there are the foundations of an arch that Augustus commissioned in 19 BC to replace the earlier one dedicated to the victory of Actium that had become politically incorrect. Immediately behind this lie the ruins of the *Temple of the Deified Julius Caesar* erected where the body of the dictator had been cremated on the site of the exedra in the front.

*The slender Corinthian columns of the Temple of Castor and Pollux*

*The Basilica Julia with the Temple of Castor and Pollux in the background, and, on the left, the Temple of Antoninus and Faustina*

# The sacred area of Vesta

Through the arch lie the recomposed ruins of the circular *Temple of Vesta*. This greatly venerated sanctuary housed the "sacred fire" that symbolized the perpetuity of the state. Its actual form dates back to the reign of Septimius Severus, but it was originally a simple hut the shape of which was imitated in this later marble structure. Beside this stands the *House of the Vestals*, the priestesses who tended the sacred fire. The present building has been altered several times. It is constructed around a rectangular courtyard with a pool in the centre that was formerly surrounded by a colonnade decorated with statues of the Greatest Vestals. Opposite stands the *Regia*, founded by Numa Pompilius, which was perhaps the residence of the Tarquins. In the Republican Era it became the seat of the *Rex Sacrorum* who, together with the *Pontifex Maximus* performed the holy rites.

## The Temple of Antoninus and Faustina

The very well preserved temple was erected in 141 AD on the death and deification of Faustina, wife of Antoninus Pius, and was also dedicated to the emperor after he died. This hexastyle and prostyle edifice stands on a high podium approached by a modern flight of steps. The 17-metre cipollin columns, still bear the grooves for the ropes dragged by oxen when an attempt was made to make them fall. The Italic-style *cella*, in *peperino opus quadratum* originally faced with marble, is decorated with a very fine marble frieze, in the cold Classical style of the Antonine period. In the 18th century it was converted into the Church of S. Lorenzo in Miranda.

*A statue of a vestal from the portico of the House of the Vestals*

*Commemorative columns on the Via Sacra with the Temple of Antoninus and Faustina in the background*

# The Basilica of Maxentius

This edifice, one of the vastest and most magnificent in Rome, was begun by Maxentius in 306 AD and completed by Constantine after 312 AD. The main entrance on the east side preceded by a narthex was subsequently moved to the south side, thus changing the orientation and hence the spectator's perception of the immense spatial volume, since the apse contained the colossal statue of Constantine, the remaining fragments of which are now in Palazzo dei Conservatori. This sculpture was an acrolith, in other words, the exposed parts were marble and the rest was of a different material. The head, with its magnetic, disquieting gaze, is 2.6 metres high. The basilica was divided into three aisles by eight pillars, with the central nave flanked by an equal number of fluted, cipollin columns, over 14 metres high, supporting a cross vault with three bays at a height of 35 metres. The only surviving column was removed by Pope Paul V and set up in front of the Basilica of Santa Maria Maggiore in 1613.

The north aisle, the only one to remain standing after the earthquake in the 9th century destroyed the building, still possesses the magnificent coffered barrel vault, over 24 metres high, that is perpendicular to the central nave and also served as a buttress for it, which impressed Renaissance artists and inspired Bramante's design for St. Peter's. Light entered through very wide windows above the nave and through the two rows of three-mullioned windows in each bay on the long sides and on the façade.

*The three large barrel vaults in the north aisle of the Basilica of Maxentius*

## The Temple of Venus and Rome

To the east of the basilica stands the Church of S. Francesca Romana, partly built on the ruins of the Temple of Venus and Rome, whose impressive remains can be seen towards the Colosseum. The size of the podium, 145 x 100 metres, make this the largest temple in Rome, together with the lost *Temple of Isis* on the Quirinal Hill. Built by Hadrian on the ruins of Nero's *Domus Aurea* in 135 AD, it was criticized by the architect Apollodorus of Damascus, who paid for this impudence with his life. This temple, surrounded by a vast peristyle of 10 x 20 columns, had two elaborate symmetrical sanctuaries placed back to back, characterized by the magnificent apse restored by Maxentius in 307 AD.

## The Arch of Titus

A well preserved stretch of road leads to the *Arch of Titus*, erected by Domitian after 81 AD in honour of his deified brother and to celebrate the victory over the Jews. This monument, which has survived because it was incorporated into the fortress of the Frangipane family, was detached and recomposed in travertine by Valadier in 1822. It consists of a single bearing arch, faced in Pentelic marble and divided by four semi-columns on each side. The reliefs on the interior representing two moments of triumph are remarkable. The one to the south shows the procession going through the triumphal gate on the right, with bearers holding up the seven-branched candlestick. In the one to the north Titus in the quadriga driven by the goddess Rome is crowned by victory, preceded by the lictors and followed by the personifications of the Senate and people of Rome. His apotheosis can be seen in the centre of the vault.

*The Arch of Titus*

*The columns of the Temple of Venus and Rome and the Colosseum*

# THE PALATINE

According to legend, Hercules and later Aeneas found a group of Greek immigrants on the Palatine. Recent finds have testified to the presence of Greek sailors and traders even prior to the colonization of southern Italy. The discovery of Iron Age huts also seems to confirm the date traditionally ascribed to Romulus's founding of Rome. From the archaic period on important religious ceremonies were held on this hill, such as the *Lupercalia* linked to fertility. In which the wolf-priests whipped everyone they met, and cults like that of the *Magna Mater* (Great Mother) or of Apollo and Vesta. During the Republic the ruling class resided here. After Augustus, who was born on the Palatine, decided to live here it became the site of the emperors' residences and increasingly vast and magnificent palaces were built. By the end of the Imperial Era the whole hill had become a vast built-up area, and the word *palatium* came to mean palace par excellence. After being abandoned for centuries, the hill was rediscovered during the Renaissance by the aristocracy who built their villas here. Towards the mid-16th century it was transformed into the extraordinary *Horti Farnesiani*, commissioned by Alessandro Farnese, and artists including Vignola and Girolamo Rainaldi contributed to their design. Very little remains of these wonderful pleasure gardens after two centuries of excavations to uncover the buried vestiges of antiquity.

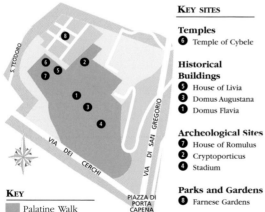

**KEY SITES**

**Temples**
❻ Temple of Cybele

**Historical Buildings**
❺ House of Livia
❸ Domus Augustana
❶ Domus Flavia

**Archeological Sites**
❼ House of Romulus
❷ Cryptoporticus
❹ Stadium

**Parks and Gardens**
❽ Farnese Gardens

**KEY**

Palatine Walk

*A reconstructed Iron Age hut with the holes for the poles*

# The Residence of Augustus

The residence of Augustus and the so-called House of Livia have been discovered in the group of late Republican houses to the south of the *Domus Tiberiana*, which has now completely disappeared. The House of Livia contains some very striking wall paintings; particularly fine are the airy landscapes in the *Triclinium* (dining-room) and the mythological paintings in the 2nd Pompeiian style in the *Tablinum* (drawing-room). The House of Augustus is divided into private apartments in that sobrely, modest style in which the *princeps* (leader) had created his public image, and rooms for official functions that were monumental and decorated with paintings of perspectives or theatrical subjects. The Greek and Latin libraries and the adjacent Temple of Apollo (built by Augustus from 36 to 28 BC) were practically connected to the villa. Augustus had transferred the statues of Apollo, Diana and Latona there, works by Scopas, Cephisodotus and Timotheus, and the valuable Sibylline Books. Opposite the house was the Temple of the Magna Mater whose non-iconic idol, that of Cybele, was imported from Anatolia in 204 BC at the height of the battle against Hannibal. That same year work began on the temple, which Augustus restored in 3 AD for obvious purposes of propaganda. Lower down to the south, protected by roofing, are the floors dug into the rock of three Iron Age huts (9th century BC) with holes for the poles to support the roof and walls, and small gutters to drain away water. According to tradition this is where Romulus lived. The symbolic link with the residence of Augustus is evident, since it is perfectly situated in a context steeped in the history of Rome.

*The Temples of the Magna Mater (left) and Victory (right)*

# The Domus Flavia

This immense Imperial palace was built for Domitian by the architect Rabirius, who incorporated some preexistent buildings into the new edifice, between 81 and 96 AD. The part used for official functions is usually known as the *Domus Flavia* and the private area that contains the stadium is known as the *Domus Augustana*. The present entrance to the *Domus Flavia* leads into a vast atrium, consisting of a rectangular peristyle with a central octagonal basin once decorated with an elaborate fountain, around which the various reception rooms are situated. To the north lies the huge *Aula Regia* where the emperor gave audiences from his throne that must have stood in the apse on the south wall. To the west is the basilica with a nave, two aisles and an apse, where law cases were discussed. The room opposite probably housed the guards near where the main entrance must have been. On the opposite side is an immense hall identified as the *Cenatio Iovis*, the extremely ornate Imperial triclinium, flanked by two smaller rooms decorated with oval fountains (nympheums) overlooked by large windows. The splendid marble pavement covers a hypocaust, probably commissioned by Hadrian, which heated the room by means of hot air flues. The size, magnificence, high ceilings, vast rooms, which must have been decorated with the most precious materials available, and sophisticated design made Domitian's palace the prototype of the residence of the *dominus et deus* based on the oriental model.

*The remains of mosaic paving in the Domus Flavia*

*The atrium of the Domus Flavia with the octagonal fountain and the triclinium*

# The Domus Augustana and the Circus Maximus

The peristyle of the *Domus Flavia* provides access to the even more spectacular peristyle of the *Domus Augustana*, which is surrounded by a four-sided portico and decorated with an extremely large pool containing an island surmounted by an idyllic temple that can be reached by a small bridge. On the south side are the private apartments, partially dug out of the hillside, a fact that has helped to preserve some rooms situated around a courtyard, flanked by nymphaeums with a basin in the centre.

The south exedra of the palace overlooks the Circus Maximus, from which the crowd could acclaim the emperor, thus significantly linking the largest area for entertainment in the ancient world to the Imperial palace, an idea that was repeated in Milan and Constantinople. According to tradition the Circus was founded by Tarquinius Priscus on the site where the rape of the Sabine women is thought to have taken place. Initially in wood, it was decorated by Agrippa who donated the seven dolphins on the central spina to mark the progress of the various laps, while Augustus erected the imperial box and the obelisk now in Piazza del Popolo. Claudius was responsible for its monumental aspect, though, according to sources, its present size of 600 x 200 metres and capacity for 250,000 - 385,000 spectators was only reached during the reign of Caracalla. In 357 AD Constantius II added a second obelisk, which now stands in Piazza di S. Giovanni in Laterano. *Biga* (two-horse chariot) and *quadriga* (four-horse chariot) races were held here and the teams of contestants could resort to any means – whether fair or foul – to eliminate their adversaries and were spurred on by an excited crowd.

*The inner courtyard of the Domus Augustana that was surrounded by private apartments*

# The Stadium and the Domus Severiana

To the east of the *Domus Augustana* is the immense sunken area of the so-called stadium. This structure dates from the time of Domitian and is shaped like a circus; it was surrounded by an imposing double portoico, dominated by the imperial box on the east side. The pillars and all the brickwork were faced with marble, the upper floor had a colonnade. One of the *metae* can be seen on the left of the arena divided by the central *spina*. It is most likely that this was once a garden and magnificent riding-ground similar to other private hippodromes discovered in the most sumptuous villas. The unusual oval enclosure seems to date from the time of the Gothic King Theodoric.

Unlike the *Domus Aurea*, which is designed like an immense villa, and the more underplayed style adopted by Augustus, Domitian's palace meets in an extremely unitary way all the political demands of an empire. The purposes of the different rooms and areas are organized within a scenographic and hierarchic framework that creates a special aura, enhanced by the exedrae, around the places where the emperor made his formal public appearances, since he had become increasingly distanced from common mortals, surrounded by a divine halo of glory, the living monument to his absolute power.

Beyond the hippodrome stand the impressive ruins of the last extension of the palace commissioned by Septimius Severus, which include the picturesque brick structures ending in a spectacular nymphaeum on three levels known as the *Septizodium*, which was destroyed in 1586 by Pope Sixtus V who wished to reutilize the marble.

*The two-storey portico that surrounded the stadium with the imperial tribune*

# The Domus Aurea

Modelled on the suburban villa, the *Domus Aurea* or Golden House was built by Severus and Celer for Nero after the fire of 64 AD, which had destroyed the emperor's earlier *Domus Transitoria*. By far the largest of the imperial residences, it occupied the vast area between the Circus Maximus, the Church of S. Pietro in Vincoli, Piazza Vittorio Emanuele II and the Coelian Hill. The surviving sector (300 x 100 metres) was used for constructing the Baths of Trajan. The chance discovery of the decorated rooms and the *Laocoön* in 1506 provided Renaissance artists with first-hand knowledge of ancient art. The excavated area consists of a large porticoed courtyard with a fountain in the centre and a nymphaeum-grotto on the east side. The group of rooms to the south, now dark and damp, included the imperial bed chamber and other rooms facing the lake below (where the Colosseum now stands). Some rooms still contain very fine paintings, now somewhat deteriorated, characterized by bright colors and dense flowing brushwork, probably executed by the celebrated Fabullus. The famous golden room, opening onto a large pentagonal courtyard, is in a poor state of repair. This leads to the octagonal room, one of the finest examples of ancient Roman architecture, which has a spherical dome without spandrels and has rooms fanning out from it including a large nymphaeum. The vestibule contained a colossal statue of Nero by Zenodorus 35 metres high, the largest bronze statue of all time. From the 8th century AD on, the amphitheatre where Hadrian placed it, after it had been given the features of Helios, was called the Colosseum.

*The room of Achilles at Sciro, the panel painted in the centre of the ceiling*

*The octagonal room in the Domus Aurea*

# The Arch of Constantine

Consisting of three supporting arches 25 metres high, this is the largest and best preserved of the Roman triumphal arches. Until a few years ago it was considered a "hotchpotch" consisting of reliefs taken from other monuments and built by the Senate as a tribute to Constantine, who had not even celebrated his victory over Maxentius. Restoration work (1982-87), however, revealed that it is a masterly work dating from the reign of Hadrian. Only the attic with the dedication to the emperor was built in the 4th century AD by using Trajan and Aurelian bas-reliefs, and reliefs depicting episodes from the life of Constantine were added. These different reliefs are an expression of the sensitivity and culture of the respective periods. The Trajan reliefs are in a vigorous, dramatic style imbued with pathos; those dating from the reign of Hadrian express a classicism "suffused with Romantic restlessness"; the Aurelian ones (from a monument erected by Commodus) display the incipient dissolution of the plastic mass into pictorial forms; while the Constantine reliefs are characterized by their anti-classical language, which is brutally expressive and roughly geometric, and developed in the tetrarchic era. Immediately to the north of the arch, recent excavations have brought to light the foundations of the *Meta Sudans*, an imposing, cone-shaped fountain dating from the reign of Flavius. Its impressive core was destroyed in 1936 to make way for Fascist parades.

*The Arch of Constantine, relief of a battle scene*

# The Colosseum

The Flavian Amphitheatre, the most famous building of ancient Rome because of its immense size and incredibly solid structure, was first built by Vespasian, who wished to return to the Roman people some of the land Nero had transformed into a lake and expropriated for his vast *Domus Aurea*. The building was not finished when he died in 79 AD and was inaugurated by his son Titus the following year with entertainments that lasted one hundred days and saw the massacre of five thousand wild beasts. Construction was completed during Domitian's reign. After the abolition of gladiator fights in 438 AD, it was still used for animal "hunts" until 523 AD. After being converted into a fortress in the Middle Ages, the Colosseum was used as a "quarry" for materials until the mid-18th century, when Pope Benedict XIV decided to convert it into the Stations of the Cross. From then on it has been restored several times, especially by Stern who reinforced the crumbling arches with a brick strut. The exterior and bearing structures are built of travertine *opus quadratum*, while the other walls are of tufa *opus quadratum*, brick and concrete. The amphitheatre is ellipsoidal in shape, with the longer axis measuring 188 metres and the shorter one 156 metres. The exterior is divided into three orders of 80 arches each framed by Doric, Ionic and Corinthian half-columns and pillars, completed by an attic storey, the total height being 48.5 metres. On the attic storey the corbels supporting the masts from which was stretched the huge awning to shade the whole arena can still be seen. This operation was carried out by a thousand expert sailors.

*A gladiator's helmet*

*The Colosseum; on the right, the colossal statue of Nero in the guise of Helios, after which the amphitheatre is named*

# The Colosseum: the interior

The 80 arches at ground level provided access to the ramps and walkways inside that led to the *vomitoria* through which the huge mass of spectators could reach the tiers of seats in orderly fashion. The numbers visible above the arches must have referred to a ticket for a particular sector. The auditorium was divided into five sectors according to the social class of the spectators (and not to the price of the ticket, since the entertainment was usually free). The lower tiers, the only ones in marble, were reserved for the senators, each of whom had the right to a named seat, then came those of the equestrian order, whereas those of the last *moenianum* that were for the plebs, who remained standing, were in wood and separated by a high wall. There was also a sector – the most unpleasant – reserved for women, after Augustus had passed a special law, since he was concerned about indiscriminate mingling of the sexes in public places leading to moral laxity. The Colosseum is estimated to have held between 40,000 and 73,000 spectators. Gladiator fights and animal "hunts" were held here, while the naval battles came to an end when the huge area beneath the arena was constructed at the end of the 1st century AD. There is no reliable evidence that Christians were martyred here, it is possible, but mention is only made of this in later legends. The arena (86 x 54 metres), separated from the auditorium by a podium and balustrade, was covered by planks of wood with trapdoors to let in the wild beasts.

*Gladiators fighting, from a sarcophagus in the Museo Nazionale Romano*

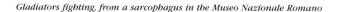

*The arena and tiered seating in the Colosseum*

# THE IMPERIAL FORUMS

The increase in population and the desire to create a complex capable of rivalling the Hellenistic capitals made Caesar decide to undertake the construction of a new forum, based on criteria that would enhance his prestige. His example was followed by Augustus, Vespasian, Nerva and Trajan, whose extraordinary forum was quite rightly acclaimed as one of the wonders of the ancient world. After the fall of the Roman Empire the area rapidly reverted to marshland and was re-urbanized from the 16th century on. The majestic ruins, slowly destroyed by the general plundering of building materials and exploited to make lime, only began to be excavated systematically in 1812. Between 1931 and 1933, the requirements of the Fascist regime, which disregarded the historic importance of the area, led to the construction of the Via dell' Impero that bisected the archaeological site and became an important artery in subsequent years. Moreover, the major objective of the excavations was to bring to light the Imperial level. The centuries-old urban fabric was replaced by a vast empty space.

The colossal *Forum of Peace*, built by Vespasian between 71 and 75 AD, is now completely buried. The medieval Torre dei Conti stands on an exedra on its perimeter. All that remains of the magnificent *Forum of Nerva* (45 x 150 metres), built in 97 AD on the rectangle remaining between the Forum of Peace and the Forum of Augustus, are two damaged architraved columns, popularly known as the "Colonnacce". The highly refined bas-reliefs above the columns, depicting Minerva protectress of craftsmen and female household tasks, testify to the quality of this complex of buildings.

*Trajan's Market, a complex of shops and offices designed by the architect Apollodorus of Damascus at the beginning of the 2nd century AD*

## The Forum of Casear

Dedicated in 54 BC and inaugurated by Caesar in 46 BC, it was completed by Augustus, extended and rebuilt by Trajan in 113 AD, and then substantially restored by Diocletian after the fire of 283 AD. This is the oldest of the Imperial Forums and served as the model for subsequent ones that copied its elongated, rectangular groundplan with the equestrian statue of the dictator in the centre, and a temple at the far end, according to a strictly axial and central-ized design. The Temple of Venus Genetrix, dedicated by Caesar in 48 BC, on the eve of the decisive battle with Pompey at Pharsalus, stood on a high podi-um approached by flights of steps on either side. It had eight columns also on each side and its fourth side was originally built up against the saddle of the Capitol. The *cella*, proba-bly vaulted and decorated with valuable columns of *giallo antico* marble, ended in an apse and housed the statue of Venus by the Greek sculptor Arcileus, in addition to many pictures and other statues dedi-cated to Cleopatra and perhaps to Caesar himself. It is likely that this layout, alien to Italic city plan-ning and based on an explicitly propagandist conception that exalted Venus Genitrix, mythical forebear of the *Gens Julia*, derived from the sanctuaries dedicated to the deified Hellenistic kings. In this regard, Suetonius recounts that Caesar had the arrogance to receive the Senate in his temple, seated like a god before the statue of Venus. Behind the double portico on the square are several tabernae and from here steps lead up to the *Clivus Argentarius*, whose beautiful pavement can still be admired.

*A bust of Julius Caesar*

*The Forum of Caesar with the Temple of Venus Genitrix*

# The Forum of Augustus

The Forum of Augustus (125 x 118 metres, built between 42 and 2 BC) is better conserved. It is possible to recognize the layout, characteristic of all the Imperial Forums, with imposing porticoes on all four sides framing a temple set on a podium at the far end. The monumental colonnades contained the statues of the *summi viri* (greatest men) of the Republic, while in the exedrae that flanked the temple those of the kings of Albalonga, Aeneas, Romulus and the Julia-Claudia dynasty were to be found, in homage to an iconographic scheme that reached its climax in the pediment of the spectacular temple, designed to celebrate Augustus as the *Pater Patriae* (Father of the Fatherland) and present him in a semi-divine light. This imposing temple, the scenographic conclusion of a space that because of its "artificiality" and richness of materials had no equal in the city of the time, was dedicated to *Mars Ultor* or Mars the Vindicator of Caesar's murder, and was dedicated by Augustus in 42 BC, on the eve of the great battle of Philippi against Brutus and Cassius. The temple, preceded by a flight of monumental marble steps, had eight columns of Luna marble 15 metres high along the front and eight along each of the long sides, of which only three remain. In the centre of the magnificent piazza stood a large statue of Augustus in his triumphal quadriga, the restorer of order and peace, the worthy heir of a very ancient tradition consecrated by the gods. Two honorary arches on either side of the temple dedicated to Drusus and Germanicus, respectively the son and grandson of Augustus, led to the back entrances to the forum in the imposing, perfectly preserved wall of rusticated blocks of dark stone 30 metres high that separated this noble area from the plebeian quarter of the *Suburra*.

*The Temple of Mars Ultor in the Forum of Augustus*

# The Forum and Market of Trajan

This immense complex of buildings (300 x 90 metres) was built for Trajan by the architect Apollodorus of Damascus who cut through the ridge between the Capitoline and Quirinal Hills. It is the last and most famous of the Roman forums and was considered the eighth wonder of the ancient world. A monumental triumphal arch provided access to the vast, porticoed piazza with the equestrian statue of Trajan in the centre. Two large hemicycles opened out on each side and were an ingenious solution for buttressing the slopes above that had been weakened by the excavation, while the last side  was entirely occupied by the Basilica Ulpia, the largest (170 x 60 metres) and most magnificent in Rome. Part of this extraordinary edifice still remains to be excavated, though some of the columns that divided it into four aisles and a central nave have already been placed upright.

The impressive market attached to the forum also served to reinforce the hill and was built on various levels based on the motif of the exedra. It is entered through an imposing two-storey hall covered in cross vaulting, which appears to have been a kind of stock market. Above stands the medieval Torre delle Milizie (13th  century) which, together with the Torre dei Conti, was the greatest in Rome.

The top floor collapsed in the 1348 earthquake. Steps lead down to the Via Biberatica with its perfectly conserved paving and lined with shops. From here one can reach the large hemicycle below, entirely in brickwork, but with the doors of the *tabernae* in travertine. The open area is dominated by the small, harmonious 15th-century loggia of the Casa dei Cavalieri di Rodi, built on the ancient ruins.

*The interior of the Basilica Ulpia*

# Trajan's Colum

From the basilica one enters a small courtyard where, flanked by two extensive libraries that have since disappeared, Trajan's Column stands. This is one of the masterpieces of all time, an extraordinary monument celebrating Trajan's victories in the Dacian wars, the booty from which was used to finance the building of the forum. The shaft that is 30 metres high consists of 25 blocks of marble 3.5 metres thick and is completely sculpted with an extraordinary spiral bas relief comprising over 2,500 figures. The brilliant, anonymous artist known as the "Master of Trajan's feats", has skilfully arranged the many episodes to meet the requirements of propaganda and dealt with the theme of war in an innovative way. Thanks to a realistic, controlled language that is both detailed and wide-ranging, the victors' successes are contrasted with the  sufferings of a heroic, proud people ready to fight to the bitter end for their freedom. The artist depicts the faces of the defeated Dacians, the horrors of war, the women and children fleeing with a pathos that has no precedent, and he succeeds in capturing, perhaps for the first time, the real man behind the enemy's mask. In the interior, a spiral staircase leads from the base, where Trajan was buried, to the top of the column where the emperor's statue was replaced by that of St Peter in 1587. The complex concluded with the temple dedicated by Hadrian  to the Deified Trajan, the size of which can be gauged from the monolithic granite column and capital lying at the foot of Trajan's Column.

*Trajan's Column*

*The lower reliefs on Trajan's Column depicting the initial episodes of the campaign against the Dacians*

# THE SACRED AREA OF LARGO ARGENTINA

The excavation of the Sacred Area of Largo Argentina in the 1920s brought to light an important complex of buildings dating from the Republican Era (3rd-2nd century BC). Four temples are visible, identified from right to left by letters of the alphabet. Remains of the original tufa pavement (2nd century BC) can still be seen under the travertine pavement laid by Domitian after 80 AD. Temple A, founded in 241 BC after the victory over the Carthaginians at the Egadi Islands, was rebuilt in its existing hexastyle and peripteral form in the mid-1st century BC, with fluted tufa columns and travertine capitals. The apses date from the 8th century AD when the small Church of S. Nicola was built on the ruins. Temple B, circular in shape and restored several times, perhaps dates from 101 BC and celebrates the victory over the Cimbrians at Vercelli; it was dedicated to "the Fortune of that day". The original columns were of tufa, faced with stucco and fluted, with travertine bases and capitals. Domitian later incorporated the columns into a continuous wall. The colossal female head discovered here, now in the Capitoline Museums, was perhaps a cult statue. Temple C, a peripteral temple *sine postico*, is the most ancient (end of the 4th-beginning of the 3rd century BC), though its present appearance results from Domitian's restoration. It was probably dedicated to *Feronia*. Temple D, the largest of the four (beginning of the 2nd century BC), is a hexastyle temple with a large *cella* and deep Italic-style pronaos; today only part of the travertine reconstruction dating from the late Republican Era is visible. Behind Temple B a large podium in tufa *opus quadratum* is all that remains of Pompey's Curia where Julius Caesar was assassinated.

*Temples of the Republican Era in the sacred area of Largo Argentina*

# THE FORUM BOARIUM

In the area of the ancient port and the *Pons Aemilius*, known today as the *Ponte Rotto*, stands the so-called Temple of Fortuna Virilis, originally dedicated to *Portunus*, the god of the port, perhaps dating from the 6th century BC and reconstructed in its present form in 2nd-1st century BC. It stands on a high podium and was converted into a church in the 9th century AD. It is a tetrastyle temple with travertine columns and a fake peristyle of tufa half-columns with travertine bases and capitals set against the *cella*. It was originally faced with plaster imitating marble. On the left side is an interesting spout in the shape of a lion's head. Nearby stands the circular so-called Temple of Vesta, originally the *Temple of Hercules Victor*, dating from the end of the 2nd century BC and extensively restored by Tiberius. It is a fine example of a marble peripteral temple (the second edifice to be built in this material in Rome) designed by a Greek architect. Its twenty columns, one of which is missing, surround a *cella* that was perhaps originally domed. It was converted into a church in the 12th century. In the area occupied by the severe medieval Church of S. Maria in Cosmedin stands the *ara maxima* (great altar) of Hercules. On the eastern corner of the piazza there is a monumental four-fronted arch, faced in marble, cross vaulted and decorated with niches, dating from the reign of Constantine. On the left of the Church of S. Giorgio in Velabro stands the small *Arco degli Argentari*, which was perhaps a monumental gate. The reliefs anticipate the sculptural developments of late antiquity in their paratactical arrangement and the hierarchy of their size.

*The Temple of Hercules Victor
better known as the Temple of Vesta*

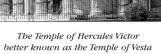

*The Temple of Portunus known as the Temple of Fortuna Virilis*

# THE THEATRE OF MARCELLUS AND THE TEMPLES OF APOLLO AND BELLONA

This imposing theatre, the only one to have survived in Rome, was begun by Caesar and completed in 11 BC by Augustus, who dedicated it to his nephew Marcellus. Extensively adapted to different uses during the Middle Ages, it was converted into a palace for the Savelli family by Baldassarre Peruzzi in 1523-27, as can be seen from the Renaissance windows in the third storey. In 1926-32 the surrounding buildings were cleared and the theatre was restored. It is very likely that it replaced an earlier, temporary wooden structure, and it reflects Caesar's desire to construct highly propagandistic works. It originally had three orders of 41 arches that reached a height of almost 33 metres and was designed to hold between 15,000 and 20,000 spectators.

The three trabeated columns standing nearby, decorated with an extremely fine frieze, are all that remains of the celebrated Temple of Apollo Medicus, dedicated in 431 BC and reconstructed in its present form in 34 BC by Gaius Sosius, who made it exceptionally refined and lavished on it extremely valuable materials. The pediment was decorated with a 5th-century BC battle of the Amazons taken from a Greek temple, while the interior of the *cella* housed other masterpieces of Classical Greek sculpture and painting, reflecting the taste typical of the "progressive" members of the patrician class. To the east are the ruins of the Temple of Bellona, built by Appius Claudius Ciecus at the beginning of the 3rd century BC. Many meetings of the Senate were held in both these buildings.

*The Theatre of Marcellus and the three trabeated columns of the Temple of Apollo*

# THE TIBER ISLAND

The Tiber Island is linked to the banks of the river by two bridges. The *Ponte Fabricio*, in an excellent state of conservation, dates from 62 BC; it is 62 metres long and 5.5 metres wide. The two large, flat arches have a span of around 25 metres. The arch on the central pier serves to permit the downflow of water. It is built of blocks of tufa and peperino and was originally faced in travertine; the present brickwork surface results from restoration work carried out in 1679. The two herms of the four-headed Janus at the ends of the parapet probably supported the bronze balustrades. The inscription in capital letters, repeated four times, records Lucius Fabricius, "*curator viarum*", as the builder of the bridge. Only the central arch of the *Ponte Cestio*, dating from the same period, now remains and has been incorporated in the 1892 reconstruction of the bridge. According to legend, the island accumulated on the grain stores that the people threw into the Tiber after the expulsion of Tarquin the Proud. The most important of the many cults that were established there was that of Aesculapius, which began when the sacred serpent of the god, borne on a ship from Epidaurus in order to chase away a plague, jumped into the river and swam to the island. This episode is represented in a travertine bas-relief on the eastern end of the island, which depicts a war trireme and Aesculapius holding a stick with a serpent curled around it (1st century BC). The Church of S. Bartolomeo was built on the ruins of the Temple of Aesculapius in the 11th century. The island is still a place of healing today, in fact the Fatebenefratelli Hospital has been located here since 1584.

*The four-faced herm on Ponte Fabricio*

*The Tiber Island with Ponte Cestio and Ponte Fabricio on the left*

# THE VIA APPIA ANTICA

The *"regina viarum"* or "queen of roads" is one of the most evocative in Rome, thanks to its ancient monuments and pleasant country setting, though this is gradually being encroached upon by building development. Opened in 312 BC by the censor Appius Claudius Ciecus, the road followed a pre-existent route and linked Rome to Campania.

❶ Tomb of
   Cecilia Metella
❷ Original paving
❸ Mausoleum
❹ Appian Fort
❺ Tomb of Marcus Servilius ❻ Tomb of Seneca
❼ Tomb of Sixtus Pompey's family ❽ Tomb of St. Urban
❾ Tomb of Caius Licinius ❿ Tomb of Hilarius Fuscus
⓫  Mausoleum of Claudius Secondinus
⓬ Tomb of Quintus Apuleus ⓭ Tomb of the freed Rabirii slaves
⓮ Tomb of Festoons ⓯ Tomb of the Pediment

Its importance is underscored by the large number and refined style of the funerary monuments and splendid villas that line it. With the advent of Christianity very important cult sites developed around the catacombs. The road was abandoned at the end of the Middle Ages and rediscovered and repaired between the 18th and 19th centuries. In 1988 it became a regional park. The *Catacombs of St. Calixtus* can be reached from *Porta San Sebastiano* and this vast, labyrinthine, subterranean complex is almost 20 kilometres long. It developed as an official cemetery of the Church on a Christian site of the 2nd century AD and contains numerous crypts, small basilicas and other architectural features, at times decorated with magnificent paintings. Further on is the *Basilica of S. Sebastiano*, which was perhaps first erected to house the bodies of St. Peter and St. Paul in the 3rd century AD; in the 4th century the martyr St. Sebastian was laid to rest there and since then the basilica has borne his name. In 1608-13 the church was reconstructed by Ponzio and Vasanzio in a simple, rigorous Mannerist style. In 1933 the ancient basilica was partially reconstructed. Steps lead down to the *Catacombs of St. Sebastian*, which contain numerous funerary rooms, some of which are painted.

*The Tomb of Cecilia Metella on the Via Appia Antica*

# THE CIRCUS OF MAXENTIUS

A little further on stands the imposing *Villa of Maxentius* (beginning of the 4th century AD. Near the Imperial palace that still remains to be excavated, stands the best-conserved circus in Rome, with its surrounding walls, towers flanking the starting stalls or *carceres* and spina – central dividing wall – from which the obelisk now in Piazza Navona was taken. Over 500 metres long and 90 metres wide it could hold around 10,000 spectators.

A very large, four-sided portico, the outer wall of which still survives, surrounds the Mausoleum of Romulus, the son of Maxentius. The tomb consists of a massive circular structure (diameter 33 metres) and a rectangular *avant-corps* that was converted into a farmhouse in the 19th century. A little further on stands the unmistakable *Tomb of Cecilia Metella*, wife of Crassus the son of the

extremely rich triumvir. This colossal mausoleum (almost 30 metres in diameter and 11 metres high) is imposing evidence of the patrician families' desire to establish their status during the last years of the Republic (mid-1st century BC). The tomb is crowned by a striking, Pentelic marble frieze depicting festoons and bulls' skulls in relief. In 1302 it was used as a tower for the nearby 11th century castle of the Caetani family.

After a couple of kilometres of road lined with the ruins of tombs, the vestiges of the huge *Villa dei Quintili* appear on the left. Building was begun on the villa in the 2nd century AD and continued in various stages. Since the 16th century great quantities of finds have been discovered here. Then comes the tomb known as the *Casal Rotondo* after the circular construction surmounting it.

*The side with the entrance and the towers flanking the starting stalls in the Circus of Maxentius*

# PORTA MAGGIORE AND THE TOMB OF EURYACES

The gate with two arches known as the *Prenestina* and *Labicana* is now called Porta Maggiore, and in fact leads to the Basilica of S. Maria Maggiore. The two monumental arches were part of the *Acqua Claudia* and *Anio Novus* aqueducts, whose impressive design was accentuated by travertine rustication, typical of the Claudian era. The gate was built on the lines of a triumphal arch on a high base, with two supporting arches flanked by three smaller openings framed by *aediculae* with tympana, the central one being reserved for pedestrians. The striking chiaroscuro of the rustication exerted a strong fascination on 16th-century architects, inspiring them to create a new, extremely popular style. The attic, which is divided into three sections horizontally to allow for the passage of the aqueducts, bears three inscriptions. The one at the top, attributed to Claudius, commemorates the construction of the gate in 52 AD, while the other two record the restorations carried out by Vespasian and Titus. It was Aurelian, however, who transformed the complex into a city gate and incorporated it into the walls he erected in great haste between 271 and 275 AD. When Honorius saw the barbarians marching on Milan in 401 AD, he strengthened the defensive structure by expanding it into massive fortifications that were foolishly demolished in 1838. In compensation, an unusual tomb in travertine from the Late-Republican Era was discovered just outside the gate. It was built by the baker Euryaces (a successful businessman and contractor who supplied the Roman army) who decorated it with round stone ovens and a frieze representing all the phases of bread-making.

*Porta Maggiore consisting of the two arches of Acqua Claudia and Anio Novus, aqueducts that brought water into the city*

# THE PANTHEON

The most well-preserved of all the Roman monuments, the Pantheon was saved because it was consecrated as a church in 609 AD. Erected by Agrippa in 27 BC, it was entirely rebuilt in its highly original present form by Hadrian between 118 and 125 AD, who conserved its ancient plan and added a portico which partly hid the circular building that closed the end of a rectangular piazza, and gallantly left the inscription attributing it to his predecessor. The building has been plundered, restored and remodelled; in fact, Bernini added two bell-towers, known as the "asses' ears", demolished in 1883. In 1870 it became the mausoleum of Italian kings. Originally, the façade was raised and the tympanum decorated with a bronze relief featuring an eagle. The colossal pronaos is made even more magnificent by sixteen monolithic granite columns 13 metres high. The wall of the *cella* is 30 metres high and 6.2 metres thick. The dome, which has a diameter of 43.3 metres, is the largest ever built in concrete; it was cast with a single pouring of cement, with a lighter pumice mixture at the top, on a wooden framework. The interior has a remarkably calm and enveloping atmosphere, which is partially due to the design based on a sphere within a cylinder (the diameter of the building is equal to its height). The circular wall is divided into seven large semicircular or rectangular niches, framed by the most beautiful pilasters and columns supporting a trabeation that terminates at the apse. The original aspect of the second order has been restored above the first exedra on the right of the apse. The dome is decorated with five concentric circles of lacunars, twenty-eight in all, that gradually diminish towards the centre marked by an *oculus* measuring 9 metres across. Raphael is buried in the Pantheon.

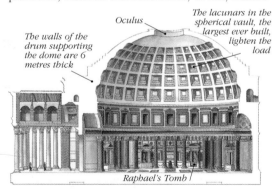

*Oculus*

*The lacunars in the spherical vault, the largest ever built, lighten the load*

*The walls of the drum supporting the dome are 6 metres thick*

*Raphael's Tomb*

*The interior of the Pantheon*

*The façade of the Pantheon*

# Hadrian's Tomb (Castel Sant'Angelo)

The tomb was begun by Hadrian and completed by Antoninus Pius in 139 AD, and used as an imperial mausoleum until Caracalla's reign. Clearly inspired by Augustus's tomb, the vast complex was originally composed of a circular cement building 20 metres high and 64 metres in diameter, covered with tufa, peperino and travertine. The marble facing was possibly decorated with pilasters surmounted by statues. Above the inner funerary chamber there was a square tower several storeys high, which culminated in a circular colonnaded temple that jutted out from the lower section, and was surmounted by a bronze quadriga with a statute of Hadrian as Helios. The enormous square base cum enclosure, added by Antoninus Pius, is approximately 90 metres long and 15 metres high and joined to the central circular construction by radial walls supporting terraces. In 271 AD Aurelian transformed the mausoleum into a stronghold and incorporated it into the city walls. This was crucial to the outcome of the Gothic Wars, and it became the key point in controlling Rome. The castle was further fortified at the end of the 14th century when it became the stronghold of temporal power and the periodic residence of the popes after their "captitivity" in Avignon. The large corner towers were added in the second half of the 15th century and raised towards the end of the 16th century, when the castle was surrounded by a daunting pentagonal rampart that was seriously damaged when the Tiber embankment was constructed. The Ponte S. Angelo is a reconstruction of the *Pons Aelius* built by Hadrian to link the mausoleum to the city.

*The statue of the angel on the top of Castel Sant'Angelo*

*Hadrian's Tomb now known as Castel Sant'Angelo*

# THE BATHS OF CARACALLA

The vast ruins of the *Thermae Antonianae* were built by Caracalla between 212 and 217 AD (the enclosure wall was actually erected by his successors and later restored several times). No other constructions were added to these baths, which are the most magnificent and well-preserved example of Imperial Roman *thermae*. They are second in size only to Diocletian's baths on which they were modelled. The baths remained in use until 537 AD when Witigis, King of the Visigoths, cut the aqueducts while besieging the city defended by the Byzantines. Built to a plan introduced in Nero's time, albeit on a smaller scale, the baths are surrounded by a monumental main wall of 337 x 328 metres, enclosing a ring of gardens in the centre of which the actual bathing complex is located. The baths were fed by a huge cistern – which is still visible – dug out of the hillside, which had a capacity of 80,000 cubic metres and was divided into 64 sections, some of which were joined. The main bathing facilities, which covered an area of 220 x 114 metres, were laid out in succession along the shorter axis, proceeding from the *natatio* (or *frigidarium*) to the basilica-like hall, *tepidarium* and *caldarium*, on either side of which two palestrae and other areas were symmetrically arranged. Excavations carried out during the centuries, and the 16th century in particular, have brought to light a vast artistic legacy, an invaluable testimony, along with the mosaics that have remained *in situ*, to the lavish decoration that adorned the baths, which were the favourite meeting place in ancient Rome for people from all walks of life.

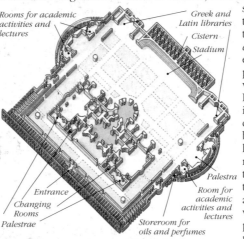

Rooms for academic activities and lectures

Greek and Latin libraries

Cistern

Stadium

Palestra

Room for academic activities and lectures

Entrance

Changing Rooms

Palestrae

Storeroom for oils and perfumes

*A plan of the Baths of Caracalla*

*The open-air swimming pool called the Natatio in the Baths of Caracalla*

# THE BATHS OF DIOCLETIAN

This vast bathing complex (380 x 370 metres), the majority of which still survives, was built by Diocletian (298-306 AD). It was able to accommodate over 3,000 bathers, and was the largest ever built in Rome. The layout was based on the customary central axis, with the *natatio*, central basilica-like hall, *tepidarium* and *caldarium* following each other in sequence. They were flanked on either side by the symmetrically arranged service rooms, changing rooms and *palestrae*. In the 16th century, Pius IV began to convert the baths into the Church of S. Maria degli Angeli, on which Michelangelo collaborated, by restoring the ancient *tepidarium*, the "basilica" and surrounding areas, and adding a presbytery with an apse. In 1750 Vanvitelli remodelled the building, installing eight brick columns in the nave and redesigning the transept. In 1911, the façade was demolished to expose the Roman brickwork: the plain façade we see today was originally the apse of the *caldarium*. The vestibule, once a part of the *tepidarium*, leads to the vast transept – formerly the basilica-like hall – with three cross vaults supported by monolithic columns, which gives one an idea of the size and magnificence of Roman baths. The octagonal hall on the left, which is over 22 metres in diameter, has been preserved almost in its entirety, while Piazza della Repubblica is an exact replica, though with a slightly smaller diameter, of the original exedra that was possibly used for theatrical performances.

*The rooms to the south of the Basilica in the Baths of Diocletian*

# THE WALLS AND PORTA S. PAOLO

Rome is the only major European city that still has ancient Roman walls, which formed part of its defences until 1870. Only a few traces remain of the earliest enceinte, attributed to Servius Tullius, and the so-called "Servian Wall" dating to 378 AD. The threat of barbarian invasion in the 3rd century spurred Aurelian to build new walls. The Emperor was able to complete the vast defensive structure, which ran for approximately 19 kilometres, in just four years (271-275) by exploiting all the constructions that could be incorporated therein and using the materials from countless buildings that were demolished. The new walls were 6 to 8 metres high. A battlemented walk with arrow slits ran along the top, and square towers with a room and windows for the archers rose up at intervals of 30 metres. The gates were the system's Achilles' heel. The major ones were twin-arched, but all gates were flanked by two semicircular towers and had an upper level where the winch for the drawbridge was located. In 401 Honorius carried out radical alterations to counter the most sophisticated assault techniques. The walls and towers were raised with salvaged materials. War machines were installed along the battlemented walk and in the towers. The gates themselves underwent extensive restructuring: twin-arches were reduced to a single arch; some gates were strengthened by an inner courtyard; the lateral towers were enlarged and raised; and many gates were actually closed. The Porta S. Paolo, formerly Porta Ostiense, still bears traces of these modifications. Nearby, the Pyramid of Caius Cestius Epulone towers skywards; the praetor built it as his tomb in 12 BC, bowing to the Egyptian fashion of the day.

*The pyramid of Caius Cestius Epulone, the tomb of a wealthy magistrate erected in 12 BC, and Porta San Paolo*

# THE AUGUSTEUM (MAUSOLEUM OF AUGUSTUS)

The mausoleum was inspired by the tombs of the great Greek kings, and more particularly the famous tomb of Mausolus, King of Caria, after which it was named. Built in 29 BC by Augustus for himself and his family, it fully conveys the significance of the dynastic policy of *primus inter pares* (first among equals). After centuries of abuse and devastation, during which the tomb was used as a fortress, travertine quarry, vineyard, garden, bull ring, theatre and concert hall, it is very difficult to reconstruct its original form. Approximately 44 metres high, the monument was originally composed of a square base enclosing a circular section on various levels, which contained a "pillar" surmounted by a bronze statute of the Emperor. The entrance was flanked by two obelisks, now on the Quirinal and Esquiline Hills. All that remains of the tomb is the lower circular wall, buttressed by a series of concentric inner walls designed to bear the load of the earth on top. The ashes of Augustus were placed in a niche in the central pillar; those of his family in the wall that surrounded it.

The *Solarium Augusti*, the largest clock and calendar ever made, stands in the vicinity. Consecrated in 10 BC, it was a giant sundial, whose gnomon-symbol of the sun was the towering obelisk that now stands in front of Palazzo Montecitorio (the lower chamber of the Italian Parliament), which cast its shadow on a complex arrangement of lines and bronze letters. On the emperor's birthday the shadow fell right on the altar of the *Ara Pacis*, to emphasize the fact that Augustus was *natus ad pacem* (born to peace).

# THE ARA PACIS

A rather uninspiring glass and cement building near the Tiber contains the *Ara Pacis Augustae* (Altar of Augustan Peace), various fragments of which were excavated from 1568 onwards. They were re-assembled in 1938, along with reproductions (accurate and recognizable) of the missing pieces. The building of the great altar was decreed by the Senate in 13 BC to celebrate Augustus's victorious return from Gaul and Spain and the ensuing peace. The altar consists of an almost square wall (11.63 x 10.62 metres) standing on a high podium, and has two entrances. The inside and outside are richly decorated with reliefs divided laterally into two sections. The decoration on the lower part features beautifully-executed acanthus volutes, embellished by swans and other animals, arranged symmetrically on either side of a cluster of plants. The upper part contains scenes recalling the origins of Rome and mythical figures on either side of the entrances; a frieze portraying the procession held during the inauguration ceremony runs around the other sides of the wall. On the right hand side, we recognize the members of Augustus's family preceded by the emperor himself (accompanied by two men wearing togas and four Flamines) with his head covered, and by Agrippa with his young son Caius Caesar. The inside panels are purely decorative. The actual altar, which stands on a high plinth, is by no means complete. The monument is a magnificent example of the stately, refined and eclectic Classicism that characterized offical art under Augustus, often cold and inexpressive.

*The expressive face of one of the figures in the side frieze of the Ara Pacis*
*The Ara Pacis and, below, the side frieze with the procession of the Julian-Claudian family*

## PICTURE CREDITS

Every effort has been made to trace the copyright holders and we apologize in advance for any unintentional omissions. We would be pleased to insert the appropriate acknowledgements in any subsequent edition of this publication.

Position of the photos on the page
t = top, tl = top left, tlc = top left centre, tc = top centre, trc = top right centre, tr = top right, b = bottom, bl = bottom le
bcl = bottom centre left, bc = bottom centre, bcr = bottom centre right, br = bottom right, c = centre, r = right, l = left

Elemond Archive 7r, 11r, 15tlc, 15bc, 15br, 35, 55

Electa Archive 23, 43, 48, 49, 93b

Giorgio Borniquez 15tr, 20, 61

Image Bank 4l, 4r, 6l, 7l, 8l, 10r, 11l, 12l, 12r, 14l, 15tc, 15trc, 21, 30, 32, 36, 42, 52, 58, 64, 71, 92, 93tr

Luca Mozzati 5, 8r, 9, 13c, 14r, 18, 25, 27, 29, 31, 33, 34, 37, 39, 45, 47, 50, 51, 53, 54, 57, 59, 63, 65, 67, 69, 73, 75, 77, 7 81, 83, 85, 87, 89

Paolo Negri 10l, 91,

Anna Serrano 13l, 26, 68, 72, 82